A NICKEL
BUYS A RHYME

A NICKEL BUYS A RHYME

Alan Benjamin

Illustrated by Karen Lee Schmidt

MORROW JUNIOR BOOKS
New York

For Ruth, Ruby, Rayanna, Rosetta,
Wray, the Reuthers, and the Roskams
—A.B.

For George Dieruf, his stories,
and our drives around Montana
—K.L.S.

Watercolors on Arches cold-pressed paper were used for the full-color artwork.
The text type is 14-point Caslon #540.

Text copyright © 1993 by Alan Benjamin
Illustrations copyright © 1993 by Karen Lee Schmidt

Printed in Singapore at Tien Wah Press.
1 2 3 4 5 6 7 8 9 10

Library of Congress Cataloging-in-Publication Data
Benjamin, Alan.
A nickel buys a rhyme / Alan Benjamin; illustrated by Karen Lee Schmidt.
p.   cm.
Summary: A collection of short poems, including "Mud Pies a
Penny," "Let's Count the Raindrops," and "Zoo's Who."
ISBN 0-688-06698-4 (trade). — ISBN 0-688-06699-2 (library)
1. Children's poetry, American.   [1. American poetry.]
I. Schmidt, Karen, ill.   II. Title.
PS3552.E5444N53   1993
811'.54—dc20   92-6475   CIP   AC

MUD PIES A PENNY

Mud pies a penny,
paper lace a dime,
three cents for lemonade,
a nickel buys a rhyme.

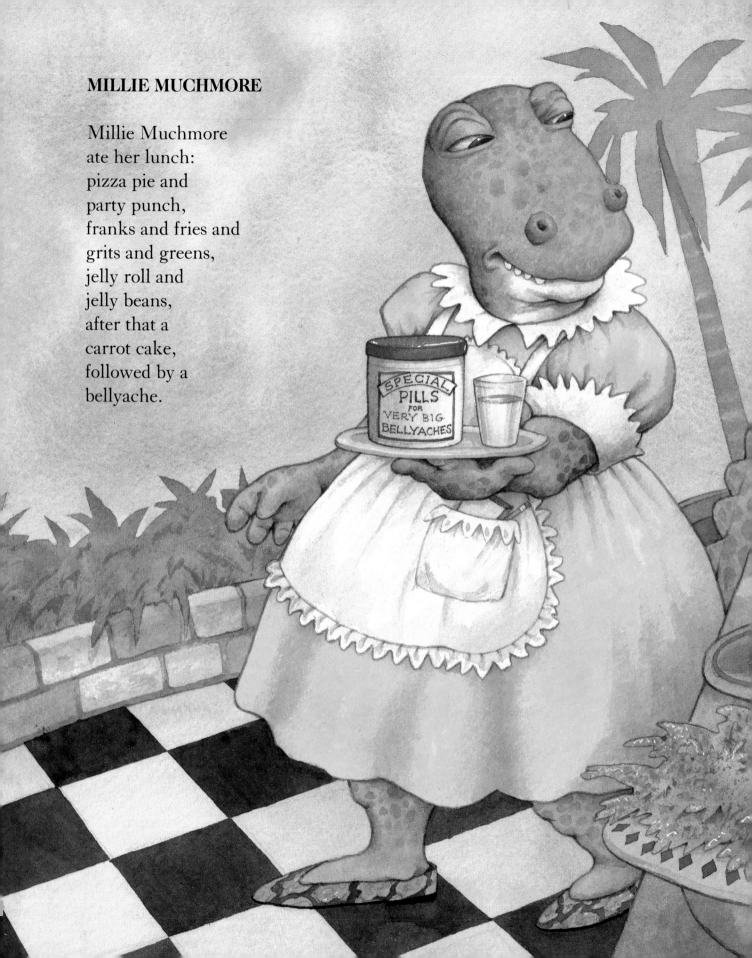

MILLIE MUCHMORE

Millie Muchmore
ate her lunch:
pizza pie and
party punch,
franks and fries and
grits and greens,
jelly roll and
jelly beans,
after that a
carrot cake,
followed by a
bellyache.

LIZA LOTT

What should we do with Liza Lott?
Claims to be what she is not.
Says that she's the Queen of Spain.
Really is a royal pain.

HELEN HIPSWAY

Helen Hipsway
did a dance,
wiggled so much
she lost her pants.

LAZY LIZZIE

Lazy Lizzie, never busy,
never cleaned her room,
never picked her clothes up,
never used a broom.

The pile grew ever higher
and wider all around,
until, I fear, poor Lizzie dear
could nevermore be found.

I'M GLAD TO SHARE

I'm glad to share
my rubber duck,
my xylophone,
my fire truck.
There's just one thing
I will not share—
my raggy, saggy
teddy bear.

FRIENDS

Billy, Willy, Milly, Mack.
Penny, Kenny, Jenny, Jack.

Annie, Manny, Fannie, Fay.
Johnny, Connie, Ronnie, Ray.

Andy, Mandy, Sandy, Sue.
Esther, Hester, Lester, Lou.

Jerry, Perry, Terry, Tim.
Bessie, Tessie, Jessie, Jim.

Eddie, Teddy, Freddy, Fran.
Molly, Polly, Dolly, Dan.

Zoe, Chloe, Joey, Jane.
Ginny, Minnie, Winnie, Wayne.

Lena, Tina, Nina, Nick.
Cora, Nora, Dora, Dick.

Stella, Della, Bella, Ben.
Harry, Gary, Larry, Len.

LET'S HAVE A PICNIC

Let's have a picnic,
with muffins and tea,
just you and your teddy,
my dolly and me.

We'll sit on a blanket,
out under the trees,
and act very grown-up
with "thank you" and "please."

RHYME TIME

Grouches grumble.
Gymnasts tumble.
Cookies crumble.
Bees bumble.
Halfbacks fumble.
Stomachs rumble.
Do *you* have any
rhymes for umble?

MAMA'S IN THE KITCHEN

Mama's in the kitchen
bakin' pies.
Daddy's on the back porch
swattin' flies.
Sister's with her boyfriend
sighin' sighs.
Brother's on the corner
tellin' lies.

MAKE A WISH

Cross your fingers
and curl your toes.
Close your eyes
and wiggle your nose.

Make a wish, but
whatever you do,
don't tell a soul
or it won't come true.

HAVE A PIECE OF FRUIT

I think that cherries
are just the berries,
that apples are
peachy, too.
And here's a pear,
so fine and fair,
a plum of a pear
for you.

EASY SEASONS

Spring's all buttercups
and breezy.

Summer's hot and
bumblebees-y.

Autumn's bright with
colored trees-y.

Winter's snowy,
sniffly, sneezy.

ONE SUNNY MAY MORNING

One sunny May morning
I planted some seeds.
I watered them daily
and pulled out the weeds.

I watered and weeded,
till one July day
I went to my garden
and picked a bouquet.

WHAT SHALL WE EAT?

Mother, Mother,
what shall we eat?
Let's bake a pudding,
warm and sweet,

with raisins and honey
and day-old bread,
some milk and eggs
from Farmer Fred.

We'll mix it up
and pat it down
and bake it till
it's golden brown.

Then, when it's time
to sit and sup,
we'll thank the Lord
and eat it up.

ONE. TWO.

One. Two.
The west wind blew.
Three. Four.
The thunder's roar.
Five. Six. Seven.
Rain from heaven.
Eight. Nine. Ten.
Sunny again.

HAPPY BIRTHDAY

Have a wonderful birthday,
a day full of cheer,
and when the day's done,
have a wonderful year.

WHAT'S FOR LUNCH?

A spider invited
a fly for lunch.

Crunch.
Crunch.
Crunch.

PRAYING MANTIS

Do you think a praying mantis
has uncles and auntis?

LET'S COUNT THE RAINDROPS

Let's count the raindrops
as they pour:
one million, two million,
three million, four.

ZOO'S WHO

Who's new at the zoo?
I'll tell you who.
The gnu is new,
and the cockatoo, too.

That the elephant house
has a very large smell
should come as no surprise,
for the wrinkly beasts
who dwell within
are of quite uncommon size.

At teatime
it's one lump or two.
With camels
it's one hump or two.

When the lion stares at me,
I have a dreadful hunch
that he sees staring back at him
a most delicious lunch.

PLANT LIFE

The dogwood's barking
in the woods.
The horse chestnut
is neighing.
The lady slipper
walks to church.
Jack-in-the-pulpit's
praying.

GUARDIAN ANGEL

Although you can't see him
when you're in bed,
a guardian angel floats
over your head.

He stays through the night
till you're awake,
and keeps you from harm
for heaven's sake.

I'M GOING TO THE PALACE

I'm going to the palace.
The queen's expecting me.
We'll sit on silken cushions
and share some talk and tea.

We'll eat leftover trifle
and speak of foreign lands.
If you would like to join us,
you'll have to wash your hands.

I'm going to the palace
to have a royal chat,
and if you want to come along,
please do not bring your cat.

The king may join us later
so if you'd like to come,
I think it would be better
not to bring your bubble gum.

I'm going to the palace.
I'd love it if you'd come.
But if you do, I must insist
you do not suck your thumb.

SUNSET

The sun has set.
The moon is bright.
Our dinner's done.
We've said good night.
We brush our teeth,
then climb the stairs,
hop into bed,
and say our prayers.

LULLABY

Under the covers,
warm and deep,
comfy and cozy,
sleep, child, sleep.

Safe in your bed
with nothing to fear,
God's in His heaven,
and Mama is here.

I LOVE TO READ

I love to find a quiet nook,
or sit beside a gentle brook,
and read a favorite picture book.
I *love* to read.

Sometimes I choose a fairy tale,
at Christmastime a merry tale,
or, if I'm brave, a scary tale.
I *love* to read.

So if you're bored and need a smile,
a trip to some enchanted isle,
just choose a book and dream awhile.
You'll *love* to read.

I THINK I'LL NEVER FALL ASLEEP

I think I'll never
fall asleep.
I've said my prayers.
I've counted sheep.
I've tossed and turned.
I've had a drink.
I've . . .

I DREAMED ONE NIGHT THAT I COULD FLY

I dreamed one night
that I could fly,
and found such pleasure
in the sky,
soaring and sailing
on the wing,
that now I know
why robins sing.

WHEN I GROW UP

When I grow up I'll have a car
to take me to the shore.
And there I'll keep a motorboat,
the ocean to explore.
And when I'm tired of land and sea,
and bored with boats and cars,
I'll hop into my rocket ship
and take off for the stars.